MASTERS OF
THE HEART ..
2nd book

By Michelle Hoover

Order this book online at www.trafford.com
or email orders@trafford.com

Most Trafford titles are also available at major online book retailers.

Note for Librarians: A cataloguing record for this book is available from Library
and Archives Canada at www.collectionscanada.ca/amicus/index-e.html

Printed in Victoria, BC, Canada.

ISBN: 978-1-4269-0734-0 (soft)
ISBN: 978-1-4269-0736-4 (ebook)

*We at Trafford believe that it is the responsibility of us all, as both individuals
and corporations, to make choices that are environmentally and socially sound.
You, in turn, are supporting this responsible conduct each time you purchase a
Trafford book, or make use of our publishing services. To find out how you are
helping, please visit www.trafford.com/responsiblepublishing.html*

*Our mission is to efficiently provide the world's finest, most comprehensive
book publishing service, enabling every author to experience success.
To find out how to publish your book, your way, and have it available
worldwide, visit us online at www.trafford.com*

www.trafford.com

North America & international
toll-free: 1 888 232 4444 (USA & Canada)
phone: 250 383 6864 ♦ fax: 250 383 6804
email: info@trafford.com

The United Kingdom & Europe
phone: +44 (0)1865 722 113 ♦ local rate: 0845 230 9601
facsimile: +44 (0)1865 722 868 ♦ email: info.uk@trafford.com

10 9 8 7 6 5 4 3 2

I am dedicating this book to the two men in my life, my father and my lifelong mate who have guided me throughout the years.

This is also for everyone who has touched me with their love and who have given me these wonderful feelings I am sharing with you today. It's all about the different aspects of love and encouraging the exploration of these facets.

It has made me the person I am today.

Below you will find the poem that titled my first book.

Matters of Our Hearts

There is no set pattern to life
There are no scripts that we follow
There is no designed path to take
There's no rule governing our heart
There is no bond taken lightly
There is no boundary to love
Mainly it's matters of our hearts

Contents

Chapter 1

---Eternal Love---

At First Sight

This is the problem and my plight
My heart was taken at first sight
No one else could compare to you
You have captured my heart so blue

Our slow dance was like pure magic
And the atmosphere electric
I knew by touch that I was hooked
When you held me close and embraced

We went our separate ways that night
To meet years later what a delight
He's free and asked me on a date
Together ever since like fate

Our lives forever entwined
Our memories enshrined
Finally as one since that dance
Our love lasting with endurance

Burning Bright

My love for you is burning bright
Like a candle lit at midnight
You take my breath away again
Like being on top of a mountain

My love for you is burning bright
With honesty and so forthright
You take me away with your charm
Your loving words to keep me warm

My love for you is burning bright
Constantly from morning to night
You take my love and set me free
To conquer battles within me

My love for you is burning bright
Even when you're out of my sight
You take me to the ends of earth
To keep me safe in our own hearth

My love for you is burning bright
Guide me in the darkness to light
You take my fears and make them sane
I've nothing to lose only gain

Every Minute of My Life

My love runs true and deep for you
As the night turns into the day
My heart aches to have you close by
Every minute of my life

You brought me here to keep me warm
You sheltered me from all the storms
My heart aches to have you close by
Every minute of my life

You taught me the ways of our life
To keep us healthy and happy
My heart aches to have you close by
Every minute of my life

Enriched with your loving presence
I will be forever endeared
My heart aches to have you close by
Every minute of my life

Foundations of Our Love

We care for each other, this is everlasting
We are good together, this is pure romancing
We understand ourselves, this is life enhancing
We trust what we believe, this is unleashed loving

We'll always belong, this isn't negotiable
We've been a couple so long, it's foreseeable
We live our lives as one, this is our best asset
We deal as one on one, this is our very best

We thrive for the future, this is the goal for us
We are enthralled by nature, this is our focus
We will live our days by the lake, this brings us bliss
We will joyfully age, this is our final wish

I have taken the time

I have taken the time
To share my feelings
To share my thoughts
To share my insight
I have taken the time

I have taken the time
To love you with all my heart
To love you unconditionally
To love you as you are
I have taken the time

I have taken the time
To take care of my loved ones
To care that everything is right
To take care that you belong
I have taken the time

I have taken the time
To give you all my love
To give you all of my respect
To give you all of my support
I have taken the time

I will always be true

It does not take me much to remember your touch
To recall those yearnings of love and the romance
I will become a friend on me you can depend
To help you to be strong make right out of the wrong
I will be your mentor rejoice your endeavours
Help you along the way to praise every day
I will always love you, I will always be true

It Is Easy To Believe

It is easy to believe in all that we hear and see
When all is right and freedom brings us all serenity
Taking life to the outmost extreme for all to partake
To love with no strings attached is all that it would take

It is easy to believe that we could work together
To build on a new foundation that we make the world better
It was always in our dreams the magic that set us free
Our feelings will conquer all obstacles when we agree

It is easy to believe that our love is meant to be
To be your spouse and friend foremost and to live life freely
A mentor to guide me to the essence of destiny
As together will live our days in tranquility

Personification of Love

You're the personification of love
You are an angel sent from above
To care for me and brighten my spirit
I feel adored through your humour and wit

You're the personification of love
As watching the graceful flight of a dove
Keeping me in your arms you set me free
To feel once more the perpetual glee

You're the personification of love
Harmonious to watch our lives evolve
Always giving when I require a hand
You're there to comfort me and understand

You're the personification of love
So free to offer your will to resolve
Providing serenity to my soul
My sacred love because you're beautiful

Remember Me

Remember me with all your heart
Until death shall tear us apart
Remember how our lives do mesh
Think of it like spring air so fresh

Remember me with love so true
Always believe in me and you
Remember who has touched your soul
As this is what will keep us whole

Remember me as we grow old
Touching and feeling as we hold
Remember all the days we've shared
Everlasting as we have cared

Remember me and the romance
Like a great choreographed dance
Remember to be by my side
United we stand out with pride

Together All of our Days

Please just give me a jump start
My heart is coming apart
I need your loving right now
With all your body and soul

Please just give me a jump start
I shall never want to part
You are the love of my life
Always shall I be your wife

Please just give me a jump start
I shall not be in the dark
Unless you are there with me
To make me safe and happy

Please just give me a jump start
My love for you is so great
The only thing that matters
Is that we're like no other

Please just give me a jump start
I need to know that you care
I need your love for always
Together all of our days

Unconditional Love

We're not perfect and we know our flaws
Everyday we enhance our lives
Together we promise to take strides
As unconditional love prevails

We continue this journey of ours
Taking and giving pleasures each day
Looking forward to the future years
As unconditional love prevails

Our love not to be taken lightly
As it has brought us laughter and tears
Together we will make it work out
As unconditional love prevails

We share our memories of the past
Reminding us of how is was then
Anticipating the rest of our lives
As unconditional love prevails

Chapter 2

---Friends and Family---

Laughing Away the Tears

You knew just what to say

To clear my mind astray

Calling a spade a spade

How to make lemonade

To tell a joke or two

To explain the why and who

And the bare logistics

So that I'll not panic

To belay all my fears

Laughing away my tears

Dedicated to my dearest friend who has been through everything
with me over the years. Thank you Anne for being there for me,
today
and always.

The Fellowship of a Good Friend

There comes a time of amity
A time of camaraderie
Time of familiarity
The fellowship of a good friend

There's the time for intimacy
There's the sociability
There's conviviality
The fellowship of a good friend

There's all the time to be friendly
All the time we're in harmony
The time of affability
The fellowship of a good friend

To Hold You Dear in My Heart

To hold you dear in my heart
To keep you near by my side
To make it clear you are loved
To stop the fear and bring calm

To hold you dear in my heart
To keep you there by my side
To make it known you are loved
To stop the hurt and bring calm

To hold you dear in my heart
To keep you next by my side
To make it said you are loved
To stop the haze and bring calm

To hold you dear in my heart
To keep you close by my side
To make it fact you are loved
To stop the ire and bring calm

Dedicated to my father with love

To Know How to Look Beyond

The time in our life has come to know how to look beyond
To find the guidance and to be able to comprehend
What life means to each and every one of us in our realm
Together we will find the meaning and ultimate calm

We will stand free to assist with the real life decisions
To ease the harsh pain of reality and short comings
We are with you today to let you know you're truly loved
Our hearts giving freely and forever we shall be moved

To find the ultimate acceptance of what life has dealt
The true meanings towards each of us and what we have felt
To realize what life has to offer and to cherish
Our memories and remember all the that is gold and rich

Together we will strive for the guidance to help the ill
To do what is in our power and our sustaining will
To bring about the everlasting love in our future
To be strong, to be loved and to find the heart to nurture

To continue with strength and guide through this time for bonding
To shower all that's dear with our exceptional loving
To be able to offer each other life's acceptance
To live to our heart's content and to find the balance

Dedicated to my loving father

To no longer feel insecure

It's been many years of pressure
To look forward to the future
I was told there would be a cure
With that I do feel reassured
To no longer feel insecure

Many a days I felt pleasure
In tune with oneself and nature
Every feeling I have nurtured
And in my heart I have treasured
To no longer feel insecure

All my feelings I have measured
My thoughts always to be censured
So my senses now feel more pure
And remember to not be lured
To no longer feel insecure

Dedicated to my dear nephew Daniel

You Are a Part of Me

You are a part of me this I know
My love shines, onto you I bestow
Just like that special star all aglow
That shall brighten the skies with its glow
To keep you sheltered within the flow

You are a part of me forever
Waiting to forge our paths together
To keep you close by when you falter
To protect you and to keep you closer
With our binding love as we gather

You are a part of me you will see
Long lasting relations to foresee
Creating a time for liberty
Lightening our days with gaiety
We are as one for eternity

You are a part of me that's for sure
To be remembered in the future
With love and laughter we shall endure
Families bonding and to nurture
The time together felt with pleasure

You Kept Me Warm

You kept me safe and warm through all of the storms
You allowed me to be the person I am now
Forever thankful for the memories bestowed
My love for you transcends into different forms
Giving me the freedom to be or to follow
As you have been forgiven and forever loved

You kept me warm and safe in times of disarray
Always understanding and counselling was free
Giving me guidance and advising as you held
You provided the love throughout the nights and days
During the tough and down times you were there for me
So strong within that I found my way in the world

You kept me warm and safe with all my endeavours
For that I've given you my gratitude and love
If not for you I would not be who I've become
We have shared our thoughts on life hours upon hours
You prepared me for the answers to life above
I shall remember that I've been always welcome

I am dedicating this poem to my father with unconditional love.
I'm always thinking of you.
With all my love from your daughter Michelle

Chapter 3

---Life---

A New Day

It is a new day to be me
It is a new day to feel free
My eyes to behold the beauty
To love nature completely

To the new day and what I'll see
Blossoms are abound openly
The scent of a flowering tree
All appear spontaneously

An oasis of green grass to see
Birds and bees eating food daily
Making nests for their family
To live for all eternity

Spring and summer brings joyfully
Earths' free painting from sea to sea
Fall and winter close subtlety
With multi-coloured scenery

Creating Reality

We are on the winning track
From side to side, back to back
We are everlastingly
Creating reality

We are pursuing our dreams
Like the summers' bright sunbeams
Our lives' intricately
Creating reality

To believe in tomorrow
Like a garden row on row
We live for all the beauty
Creating reality

Our plans' logical process
Bringing happiness to us
Caught in perpetuity
Creating reality

It's what personifies all that we are

We have a distinctive identity
We have our individuality
We have a particular uniqueness
We have our very own exclusiveness
It's what personifies all that we are

There are no two identical persons
There are no explanations or reasons
There is no one land as we're national
There's no one alike insurmountable
It's what personifies all that we are

We're special having our own perspective
We are unequaled in the way we live
We are blessed with various characters
We represent life of our forefathers
It's what personifies all that we are

Magical Days and Nights

Should be a time to remember
Our vacation filled with splendour
Cherished on the return flights
All those magical days and nights

Pictures of sunrises and sunsets
The beautiful people we've met
All those unbelievable sights
All those magical days and nights

The food and the drinks the mainstay
Swimming and tanning each day
It's time to rest and clear our lists
All those magical days and nights

My Inner Smile

I've lost my precious inner smile
It' has been hiding for awhile
Hoping for it to return soon
I'm saddened without its cocoon

Just to bring back my inner smile
I would run a marathon mile
Forever grateful when it's back
To put me back on the right track

When I locate my inner smile
It shall compliment my profile
I'll need to be calm and happy
To have my own sanctuary

I've experienced my inner smile
This has kept me going for now
I'm anxiously waiting the day
When my inner smile's here to stay

New Beginnings

There is a first time for everything
To learn the ways of life that will enhance
Our day to day living with endurance
It is time to start our new beginnings

There is a place and time for forgiving
To put behind the days of denying
To take charge and to now be controlling
The things that we do for new beginnings

Listen to your heart and keep following
The trails of a time and experience
To guide your future and your existence
Capable to foresee new beginnings

The Power

The power behind the wheel
The power within our hands
The power we yield so free
The power that guides us all

The power of intellect
The power beyond our minds
The power governing self
The power that calls to us

The power to conquer love
The power of our heart beats
The power all consuming
The power that gives us life

The Rhythm of Life

It's everywhere in our heart and mind

It shows that we care and it's ours to find

It appears to us in different ways

Sometimes in disguise in all of our days

We're the same as the purpose is clear

Each arrow we aim finds our heart so dear

We love and we live to find our rhythm

We share and we give as life's the reason.

Top Ten Ways to Feel Love

First – It begins when you are born

Second – It begins when you can talk

Third – it begins with your first smile

Fourth – it begins with your first steps

Fifth – it begins with your first crush

Sixth – it begins with your first date

Seventh – begins when you love yourself

Eighth - begins on your wedding day

Ninth – begins when you love your spouse

Tenth - it begins with your first child

Happy Family Day!!

Whatever life brings me

Whatever life brings me I hope I will feel free
It's been twenty long years I have shed all my tears
I've struggled to stay well even though it's been hell
I've survived day by day wishing it goes away
With help I've stayed alive for good health I will strive

Whatever life brings me I hope I shall be free
Doing what I can do always thoughtful and true
Taking care of myself so that I'm set for life
Aspire for happiness live life to the fullest
Take care of family and keep looking forward

Whatever life brings me I hope I shall be free
Bringing laughter to all so that I shatter the wall
Always thinking of ways to brighten all my days
Living to seek wellness I continue my quest
To find that special place when I will live in peace

Written Upon The Stars

No matter what our plans are or our perceived wishes

There is the element of change that will guide our lives

The passage within our range that governs all of our days

So we continue living our planned destiny

To remember all the people passing in our life

That will forever hold a special spot in our hearts

The journey of our life is written upon the stars

Chapter 4

---Of Lost Love---

Heartbreaker

We have all been through it at least once in our lives
Our hearts taken away to never be alive
Waiting for a new romance to again arrive
Our emotions crushed by our dear loved heartbreaker

We have moved along now to a different tune
Letting go the memory and our spirits bloom
To continue our search for the perfect one
And to let go of the past left by our heartbreaker

We now begin a new search with our soul intact
To again forge ahead to find our lifelong mate
To seek the everlasting peace that comes with fate
And say a final goodbye to our heartbreaker

Jump Start Your Heart

I'm comatose and feeling that I've lost
My heart is broken at an untold cost
No one's to blame just try to forget the name
Move on to know again that special flame
Take a new route and jump start your heart

Let go the past and remember always
The good memories in your special ways
Savour the calm with joy and graciousness
Take with you all that is dear and precious
In your own special time jump start your heart

Begin anew to find the perfect mate
Remind yourself that it's never too late
There is someone out there for each of us
Life is just too beautiful and precious
You will know when to jump start your heart

You've Torn My Heart Apart

I think of you always
For years, months, weeks, and days
It seems like yesterday
That we parted our ways
It was love from the start
You've torn my heart apart

I hope your life is fine
Compared to an aged wine
Forever on my mind
You are one of a kind
It was love from the start
You've torn my heart apart

I will try to believe
That it was right to leave
The choice that sealed our fate
For which we still regret
It was love from the start
You've torn my heart apart

Chapter 5

---French Poems---

C'est Le Temps

Quand tu êtes toujours là pour moi
Avec un sourire et ton amour
Quand tu m'embrasse et dites bonjour
C'est le temps que j'aime pour toujours
C'est t le temps

Quand tu me donnes l'encouragement
Pour continuer comme avant
Avec la grâce de certainement
C'est le temps que j'aime pour longtemps
C'est le temps

Quand tout me fais croire en moi-même
Et j'ai la confiance que j'aime
Ma vie soit remplie avec un sense de calme
C'est le temps que j'aime pour un millenium
C'est le temps

Quand vous êtes mon meilleur ami
Et on communique jour et nuit
Ça me montre qu'on est uni
C'est le temps que j'aime pour toute ma vie
C'est le temps

Je me souviens

Je me souviens des bons moments
Je me souviens avec tout mon coeur
Je me souviens des joyeux temps
Je me souviens avec tout mon amour
Je me souviens

Je me souviens des heures de plaisir
Je me souviens avec tout mon coeur
Je me souviens quand tu m'as fait rire
Je me souviens avec tout mon amour
Je me souviens

Je me souviens des heureuses années
Je me souviens avec tout mon coeur
Je me souviens des jours distingués
Je me souviens avec tout mon amour
Je me souviens

Chapter 6

---Searching For Love----

I No Longer Have to Search for Love

It seems I have been looking in all the wrong places

I thought there would be a feeling like the thrill of races

Like the excitement on a first date and first kiss

I've been so worried because I expected the bliss

Now I know it's always been in my heart to see

I no longer have to search for love it's found me

Love Will Find You

Open your heart and love will find you

Don't look for love as love will guide you

Open your eyes and feel your senses

Believe in yourself and your senses

You'll know when the right one comes along

It's what you were looking for all along

Exemplifying all that's virtuous

Your future planned so virtuous

Let nature unfold in terms of love

Then you'll know the true meaning of love

Victims of Love

There is no way to predict our feelings
And know that it will be everlasting
There are no two relationships the same
And that we've all been victims of this game

There's the fact we cannot live without it
It binds us together as one unit
There's such a magnitude of importance
Placed on us to find the love and romance

There are drawbacks not to have someone dear
To share with you the laughter and be near
There's the chance you'll meet that special one
The one you were seeking in the million

There is the chance that we take which may fail
To being a victim to no avail
There's always different ways to look at it
But our heart remains to be the target

Chapter 7

---Stress Relievers---

Just Kill Me Now

I'm not ready to commit
I've been feeling lost a bit
I'll need to use all my wit
Just kill me, just kill me now

I'm not sure of my future
I've still got months to ponder
I'll need a little longer
Just kill me, just kill me now

I'm not coping there's no doubt
I've got to protect my health
I'll play the cards as they're dealt
Just kill me, just kill me now

I'm preparing for the worst
I've picked the funeral's hearse
I'll do my insurance first
Just kill me, just kill me now

I'm giving it my all still
I've worked hard to make a deal
I'll be renewing my will
Just kill me, just kill me now

Just Lock Us In

His lips on mine, skin to skin
Sweet surrender I give in
Ooh la-la, oh my, he's mine
Just lock us in, lock us in

His lips on mine, skin to skin
Let's start over, re-begin
And to play to win, win, win
Just lock us in, lock us in

His lips on mine, skin to skin
Together are hearts akin
Our future will now begin
Just lock us in, lock us in

His lips on mine, skin to skin
Forging paths with discipline
Take away the restriction
Just lock us in, lock us in

P.M.S

1. P.M.S *(Pretty Much Sucks)*

P.M.S. those three little letters
Carry such a load on our shoulders
P.M.S. what does it really mean?
Don't know 'bout you but I could just scream

2. P.M.S *(Powerful Mood Swings)*

P.M.S. those three little sayings
Contains a power house of feelings
P.M.S. brings on the tears and sweats
Like a waterfall totally wet

3. P.M.S *(Please Make Sense)*

P.M.S the three little combo
That makes us more in tune with Rambo
P.M.S reveals our inner voice
The sarcasm and wit sounds like advice

4. P.M.S *(Perfect Male Species)*

P.M.S the three little mad mix
To the doctor for our monthly fix
P.M.S brings on insanity
God help those who pass the boundary

Take a Step Back

When you are no longer in control
The world and the planets on a roll
It's time for you to take a step back
Gather yourself and get back on track

You will soon find the silver lining
Your problems are no longer stressing
It's time for you to take a step back
Look towards the stars as white and black

You will soon be laughing not crying
The days and nights you will be guiding
It's time for you to take a step back
As the person in you shall attract

There'll be no shoulders to cry upon
Only hands to grasp and to hold on
It's time for you to take a step back
To find the way you no longer lack

You're Killing Me

Up at five to start my day
Dress for the upcoming day
Drive in rush hour traffic
Getting there a miracle
You're killing me, killing me

Deadlines we're there to try and meet
To excel each moment a feat
Together we're all up a creek
Working to complete week by week
You're killing me, you're killing me

I truly try to do my best
And want perfection in each task
So we all continue to strive
To stay healthy and recognize
You're killing me, you're killing me

I keep up with the current work
To meet my objectives each week
But there's a backlog on my desk
And it's not going away quick
You're killing me, you're killing me

It's just a normal day for me
Cope with stress and anxiety
Play music to alleviate
Looking for the joy in my fate
You're killing me, you're killing me

Chapter 8

---True Emotions---

Emotions

When your thoughts take you over and there's no spice or clover
Trying to control your life with happiness and kindness
Wondering how it happens, how there hasn't been no end
To self made mockery can there not be a way to be
I'm in a predicament and cannot find enjoyment
I am in need to feel strong, to play my favourite song
To once again feel at peace to find my very own niche
So that there will be closure and again to feel pleasure
To disregard my notions to conquer my emotions
To believe in the romance in the solid permanence

Fly With Me

Fly to the ends of the earth with me
We'll soar in the skies for liberty
Take our love and create history
So we prevail to expand all seas
Fly with me

Fly the universe to feel peace
Begin our journey when the stars dance
In unison we will find romance
To keep us strong and give endurance
Fly with me

Fly throughout the world at our pace
So we freely range from place to place
To look upon the wonders with grace
To be free again to now feel safe
Fly with me

Fly to touch the celestial stars
Fly to release confinements once more
Fly so we can reopen the door
Fly amongst the people we adore
Fly with me

I am reaching out

- I am reaching out to find my true love
I am reaching out to the one above

- I am reaching out to meet my loved one
I am reaching out to find that someone

-I am reaching out and hope it is fate
I am reaching out to meet my life mate

- I am reaching out to rid me of tears
I am reaching out to be yours for years

-I am reaching out to feel whole again
I am reaching out to remove the pain

I am reaching out

I Don't Know Why

I'm hot then cold, I'm shy then bold
I laugh then I cry I don't know why
I'm down then glad, I'm well then sad
I sing then I cry I don't know why

I'm bad then I'm good, I'm sand then wood
I care then I cry I don't know why
I'm fast then tired, I'm slow then wired
I smile then I cry I don't know why

I'm here then gone, I'm up then prone
I live then cry I don't know why
I'm near then far, I'm light then star
I love then cry I don't know why

If I Just ...

If I just put my mind to it
Everything would be perfect
If I just put my mind to it
Everything I could predict

If I just knew what that was
Everything would have a cause
If I just knew what that was
Everything I'd realize

If I just took a deeper look
Everything's clear as a brook
If I just took a deeper look
Everything opens like a book

If I just could have some patience
Everything would make more sense
If I just could have some patience
Everything would be in place

If I just took all the advice
Everything at a steady pace
If I just took all the advice
It wouldn't be such a rat race

It's Time to Heal

It's a time of rejuvenation
It's a time of recollection
It's a time of regeneration
It's a time of salvation
It's a time of healing

It's a time to wonder
It's a time to ponder
It's a time to remember
It's a time to conquer
It's a time to heal

It's a time for caring
It's a time for sharing
It's a time for loving
It's a time for forgiving
It's a time for healing

Life's Journey

When you begin to accept yourself
Life's journey takes a wonderful turn
All is pleasant and serene once more
And it is like a wonderful dream
Stress will no longer be a factor
And peaceable becomes your psyche
It will be a brand new beginning
It is the course of your life's journey

It is coping with reality
And to perceive yourself trustworthy
To realize your own destiny
And to cherish all of your family
Shows us how endearing love can be
When sharing it for eternity
It is a new start when you can see
The passage of one's own life journey

It's reaching out to all the people
Who have partaken within your realm
To telling and showing them they're loved
And to letting all your dreams unfold
To caring with loving tenderness
And kindness so there's no more worry
It is showing them how you can walk
The soulful pathway to life's journey

Simple Ways of Giving

Sometimes it's just a kiss or just a hug
Sometimes it's just going that extra mile
Sometimes it's sharing coffee in a mug
Sometimes it's good advice or just a smile

Sometimes it's sharing a laugh or a joke
Sometimes it's making peace and loving you
Sometimes it's just the feelings you evoke
Sometimes it's caring when someone is blue

Sometimes it's a simple phone call away
Sometimes it's crying on someone's shoulders
Sometimes it's just to show them the right way
Sometimes it's complementing endeavours

Sometimes it's just being you and loving you
Sometimes it's helping anew and living
Sometimes it's just keeping an eye on you
Sometimes it's just simple ways of giving

Strength (To Carry On)

There was a time when all would rhyme
There was a time when all was in decline
There was a day when all would play
There was a day when all was in disarray
There was an hour when all would be in power
There was an hour when all was in sheer horror
There was a minute when all would unite
There was a minute when all was not right
There was a moment when all would comment
There was a moment when all was dormant
There was a second when all was pretend
There was a second we all comprehend
There is the present when all have strength
There is the present when all is excellent

Take Me Faraway

It's been a long five days and I've worked for my pay
I'm headed to my home I thank the Lord I'm here
The weekend has arrived, my calendar is clear
Now it's time to revel, so take me faraway

Time to sleep in, to relax and enjoy the day
To rejuvenate and spend time with my loved one
To prepare the weeks ahead and to just have fun
Now it is time to play, so take me faraway

Time to return to work and I am on my way
Pondering the good times and my untold future
I can't wait for the week to end and start over
Now it's time to exert, so take me faraway

The Beauty Surrounds Us

The beauty of nature is all around me
I will soon stop to appreciate it, you'll see
The beauty also lies in the deep blue sea
I will soon take the time for fun, you will see

The beauty displays itself everyday
I will soon take a break to look, you will see
The beauty will always take my breath away
I'll soon be able to attest to that, you'll see

The beauty of our universe in the stars
I will soon stay awake at nights, you will see
The beauty in the sky like the moon and Mars
I will soon be on vacation, you will see

The beauty of the sunshine and healing rays
I will soon open all my doors, you will see
The beauty abounds and takes our breath away
I will soon have time to take a minute, you will see

The Passage of Time

I ponder on the past and the future
And the people who've influenced my way
Remembering the good with the bad times
Sharing in the happiness and laughter
Together we've shaped our path every day
With those we've encountered in our lifetime

How to express all of the sensations
For those around me who've inspired me
They've given their love and care so sublime
Evermore hold them close with emotions
To never be forgotten in memory
To reminisce in the passage of time

The Treasure

I have been in pain for so long
I can't remember what went wrong
The days and nights just string along
I must remember to be strong

It's been many roller coasters
On which again my mind falters
Thinking of ways to find shelters
Put in prospective the factors

It has been many years ago
That I felt my emotions flow
To care once more my heart aglow
To brighten like a new rainbow

It's taken a toll that's for sure
My feelings so sacred and pure
To again feel all the pleasure
To be given back the treasure

To no longer having regrets

It has taken me a while to no longer have regrets
To be happier than sad if I could just not forget
My life would be less stressful if I tried to let them go
And ensure the good times outweigh the bad ones then you'll know

It has taken me a while to no longer have regrets
To be happier than sad if I could just not forget
To leave the past and my thoughts, to keep just a memory
To no longer misconstrue and shed the weight I carry

It has taken me a while to no longer have regrets
To be happier than sad if I could just not forget
The love, sharing and caring, the happiness and laughter
All these feelings have brought back my long lost smile forever

What Will It Take

When everything just goes all wrong
And your thoughts are spinning all around
It is not the time to step backwards
But to stand stronger and look onwards
To take it day by day in your stride
Always living life to the fullest
What will it take to give it your best?

When everything is not just right
And there may be no relief in sight
It's time to buckle down and stay safe
And to put on a brave, loving face
All will come together and bring peace
What will it take to feel the romance?

When things finally falls into place
And we are following our life's pace
It's time to step forward and claim your rights
And think of the love within our sight
To follow all of your hearts' yearnings
What will it take to speak our feelings?

Chapter 9

---Wedding Vows---

I'll be there for you

I'll be there for you when you need a hand
I will understand, together we stand
I'll be there for you when you call my name
From night until dawn when anxious or calm

I'll be there for you to support your dreams
Through good and bad times as we are a team
I'll be there for you with each breath you take
And make no mistake when life is at stake

I'll be there for you, together we've won
Bringing joy and fun when life comes undone
I'll be there for you 'til the end of life
Through famine and strife as your friend and wife

It's Inevitable

Our hearts do lovingly entwine
We are like the midday sunshine
We are one another's life line
It's inevitable you're meant for me

Our thoughts are lovingly sincere
Our paths united it is clear
We are connected there's no fear
It's inevitable you're meant for me

Our lives are lovingly ardent
It has been since the commencement
Our feelings growing month by month
It's inevitable you're meant for me

Lasting Love

I never really knew who you were
It was moving and something like fate
You soon touched my heart like no other
When you asked me out on our first date

You treated me like I was special
We discussed our past and future
Discovered we were compatible
Our new found feelings to be nurtured

Together we'll find our tomorrows
Forging ahead with our own passage
Taking paths we're compelled to follow
Like a book unfolding page by page

Memories will soon be created
Our life to never be forgotten
Love to sustain us as we have lived
To share our lifetime had been chosen

Love Is Eternal

- When you look at me with love in your eyes
I will not forget love is eternal

- When you look at me with adoration
I will remember love is eternal

- When you look at me with all that is you
I will keep in mind love is eternal

- When you look at me with care and longing
I'll always recall love is eternal

When you look at me with your heart so pure
I will always feel love is eternal

My Love

My love transcends all seas
My love climbs all mountains
My love drives all terrains
It's there for all to see

My love flourishes with one look
My love shines like a new sunbeam
My love takes life to the extreme
It's there like a well written book

My love expands all the wakening skies
My love is unreserved with honesty
My love is pure like a new born baby
It's there to be looked upon by the wise

My love is the splendour of an opening bloom
My love is a gift to you for all of my life
My love takes on a new beginning as your wife
It's there to capture and share like a bride and groom

Partnerships

Your instant acceptance of who I am
You're giving ways and thoughts were like a dream
The attraction immediately felt
Our love for one another the result

You have truly brought to us salvation
Your guidance giving us liberation
With your selflessness a destination
Your caring inspires my devotion

We have the ability to foresee
The know how to plan out our destiny
We have the mastery to comprehend
We have a partnership until the end

So simple yet so profound

Our love so simple yet so profound
Our heart beats govern how we are bound
Together coupled and stand as one
Truly we're blessed and have bet and won

Our lives so simple yet so profound
Encases the love by which we are bound
Together we are a team in tune
Truly a gift that's brought us fortune

Our love so simple yet so profound
Creates history by which we're bound
Together we share wondrous feelings
Truly we've found the gift of being

Our lives so simple yet so profound
The candid trust by which we are bound
Together our devotion endured
Truly love has sustained and matured